Savannah

A PHOTOGRAPHIC PORTRAIT

PHOTOGRAPHY BY

DEBBI ZEPP

NARRATIVE BY

KAREN T. BARTLETT

First published in the United States
of America by:

Twin Lights Publishers, Inc.
8 Hale Street
Rockport, Massachusetts 01966
Telephone: (978) 546-7398
http://www.twinlightspub.com

ISBN: 1-885435-85-1
ISBN: 978-1-885435-85-9

10 9 8 7 6 5 4

(opposite)
Once the grand entrance to a
Southern plantation, this azalea-
lined avenue of oaks shades the
monuments and gardens of Bonaventure Cemetery.

(frontispiece)
Forsyth Fountain

(jacket front and back)
Bonaventure Cemetery

Narrative by Karen T. Bartlett
www.karentbartlett.com

Book design by:
SYP Design & Production, Inc.
www.sypdesign.com

Printed in China

$\mathcal{OS}$avannah: as languid as a glass of fine sherry; as mysterious as a secret garden behind wisteria-draped walls. She's as dignified as the stone lions that stand sentry before many of her historic landmarks; as fanciful as the curlicued fretwork of Victorian architecture. She's spiritual and reverent: Savannah is home to some of the most beautiful churches in America, and one of the most beautiful and historic cemeteries in the Western world. She's a gracious and well-mannered lady, but prissy she's not. To prove it, drop into town (along with 400,000 other visitors) on St. Patrick's Day, when the *wearin' o' the green* means green hair and green beer; when even the Savannah River and the park fountains run green.

Savannah is a city of *firsts, oldests* and *home-ofs*: the first steamship to cross the Atlantic… home of the Girl Scouts of America… Georgia's oldest African American community… the oldest portable steam engine in the United States. John Wesley preached his first sermon in America here, and native son Johnny Mercer wrote "Moon River" here.

Savannah is where your shrimp comes right off the boats, and no self-respecting breakfast is served without a bowl of buttery grits. Nowhere can you taste a better pecan pie or dine so well on fried chicken and all the fixin's, including cornbread made properly in a cast iron skillet. But Savannah also is the city of fine cuisine in gracious dining rooms. The city continues to attract renowned chefs from around the world.

Savannah lays claim to one of the most notorious true murder mysteries of the 20th century, complete with a cast of characters and locations enough to spawn several tour companies.

Some of the finest examples of 18th- and 19th-century architecture in America lie within the Historic Landmark and Victorian Districts, where elaborate gingerbread houses blend harmoniously with imposing Georgian, Greek Revival, Gothic, English Regency, and Federal designs by famed architects John Norris and William Jay.

We invite you to savor these images of Savannah: horse-drawn carriages, gracious bed and breakfast inns, street musicians, showy Formosa and Tabor azaleas as big as salad plates, ghost stories, gas-lit cobblestone streets, and massive oak trees drenched in Spanish moss and more. We hope this collection of evocative photography by Debbi Zepp will compel visitors to return; and remind those lucky enough to live here why they never want to leave.

Orleans Square

Orleans Square, located near the Savannah Civic Center, commemorates the War of 1812 Battle of New Orleans and honors commander General Andrew "Old Hickory" Jackson. The square also features the German Memorial Fountain, which pays tribute to Savannah's early German immigrants.

Bonaventure (above)

A former Southern plantation, Bonaventure Cemetery overlooks the Wilmington River and the golden marshes of St. Augustine Creek. It is the final resting place of Pulitzer Prize winner Conrad Aiken, Savannah-born lyricist Johnny Mercer and many well-known Savannah families.

Little Gracie (opposite)

Among the most captivating Savannahians was the six-year-old child of a prominent hotelier. Little Gracie Watson died of pneumonia in 1889, and this monument by John Walz at Bonaventure still captures the hearts of all who see her. Some claim her spirit still lingers and that her laughter can be heard at the site of the old Pulaski Hotel.

Angels and Cherubs

Beneath the serene smiles and gentle tears of hand-carved angels and cherubs are group burials of the Order of Railroad Conductors, veterans of the Spanish American War and both World Wars, and the ashes of 344 Holocaust victims. Jewish burial customs are preserved in a section purchased by Congregation Mikve Israel.

Bonaventure Cemetery *(above and pages 10–11)*

Once a working plantation, Bonaventure Cemetery, with its serene paths, wrought iron gates, and beautiful Victorian-era stone and marble sculptures, is among the most beautiful cemeteries in the world.

Tritons and Swans *(above and opposite)*

Among the most notable urban parks in America, 20-acre Forsyth Park straddles the Historic and Victorian Districts. Its design in 1858 was influenced by the broad boulevards of Paris, and its centerpiece, with spouting swans and tritons, is a stunning fountain modeled after the twin fountains at *Place de la Concorde.*

Forsyth Park Tradition

A time-honored Savannah tradition has brought generations of families to stroll beneath the ancient oak trees after church or synagogue, and to pose for springtime family portraits against the park's massive azalea bushes.

Promenades and Benches

At pleasant intervals along the brick promenades are old-fashioned park benches—the perfect spot for reading and people-watching, or to share a bag of roasted peanuts with the friendly squirrels.

Dogwoods Heralding Spring

Savannahians know it is really springtime when the first dogwoods present their snowy blossoms in the squares and gardens, and along the riverbanks throughout the county.

Fragrant Garden

With its expansive shady lawns, Forsyth Park is a popular venue for free jazz concerts, symphonic concerts, and the annual Shakespeare Festival. The white columned building tucked into the azaleas is part of the Fragrant Garden for the Blind.

Wright Square (opposite)

This imposing monument honors William Washington Gordon, the founder of the Central of Georgia Railroad. Wright Square, located at Bull and President Streets, has a poignant ghost tale involving the first woman to be hanged in Georgia, and it is the final resting place of Yamacraw Chief Tomo-Chi-Chi.

Big Duke (above)

Big Duke is a landmark that has been familiar to Savannahians for more than 100 years. Originally it was used as a fire alarm, and later to announce momentous events, including the end of the Spanish American War. In 1985 it was rededicated as a memorial to "firefighters of all nations."

Calhoun Square

Calhoun Square, on Abercorn Street, was one of Savannah's last squares built under the plan laid out by General James Oglethorpe in 1733. It was named for Secretary of War John C. Calhoun, who later became Secretary of State and also served as Vice President of the United States under John Quincy Adams and Andrew Jackson.

Chippewa Square

The statue of Georgia's founder, General James Oglethorpe, presides over Chippewa Square, and, surprisingly, not over the nearby square that bears his name. The renowned park-bench scene from *Forrest Gump* was filmed here. The bench now resides at the Savannah History Museum.

Fountains, Benches, and Flowers *(above)*

The squares of Savannah were designed, European-style, as shady parks for the homes and churches which would be built around their perimeters. Here, Johnson Square maintains the ambience of this gracious Old-World city. The water of the fountain is tinted emerald green in celebration of St. Patrick's Day.

Jasper Monument *(opposite)*

This impressive monument in Madison Square honors Sergeant James Jasper, war hero in the 1779 Siege of Savannah. Named for President James Madison, the square also features a cannon marking the starting point of one of Georgia's first roads.

Columbia Square (top)

Facing the historic Davenport House, Columbia Square's focal point is the Wormsloe Fountain. Often referred to as the "rustic fountain," it was relocated from the ruins of Wormsloe, one of Georgia's first plantations.

Johnson Square (bottom)

One of Savannah's original city squares, Johnson Square was named for the early 18th-century Governor of South Carolina, Robert Johnson. In 1860, the Secession Flag was unfurled here from the monument to Revolutionary war hero General Nathaneal Greene, George Washington's second in command.

Ghosts and John Wesley (opposite)

According to the tellers of ghost tales, Reynolds Square is one of Savannah's most likely haunted places. They say the center of the square once was used to burn the bodies of malaria victims, whose ghostly presence still lingers after dark. The monument honors John Wesley, founder of Methodism.

Wright Square (above)

Named for Sir James Wright, the last colonial governor of Georgia, this square reportedly has its own ghost. Here, a female servant was hanged, immediately after giving birth, for the murder of her abusive employer. She is said to wander the square in broad daylight, asking people to help find her baby, only to disappear before their eyes.

Romantic Whitfield Square (opposite)

The charming Victorian gazebo in Whitfield Square is a romantic spot for weddings. The square, on Habersham between Taylor and Gordon Streets, is presided over by the beautiful gothic First Congregational Church.

Chief Tomo-Chi-Chi

The giant granite boulder in Wright Square
honors Creek Indian Chief Tomo-Chi-Chi, who
governed the town of Yamacraw before it was
"discovered" by General James Oglethorpe
in 1733. Tomo-Chi-Chi served as a mediator
and became a close friend of Oglethorpe.
The boulder replaced the original mound
of rocks called the Pyramid of Stone.

Cherubs and Balustrades

The grace and charm of Savannah lies partly in its rich treasures of architectural art, from elegant marble-and-stone entryways to garden statuary. Much of the period art was brought on great ships from Europe in the 18th and 19th centuries; other pieces have been crafted by fine artisans to reflect the bygone era.

Lafayette Square *(above)*

The Colonial Dames of Georgia presented the city with this fountain, commemorating the 250th anniversary of the founding of Savannah. The square was named for Revolutionary War hero Marquis de Lafayette. Located on Abercorn Street between Harris and Charlton Streets, it faces the Cathedral of St. John the Baptist.

Monterey Square *(opposite)*

Another Revolutionary War hero, General Casimir Pulaski, is honored in this square, bordered by some of Savannah's finest architecture. The most famous home on Monterey Square is the Mercer Williams House, around which the true story of *Midnight in the Garden of Good and Evil* revolves.

Colonial Cemetery

There's a life about this centuries-old cemetery in Savannah's Historic District, from the cadence of passing horse-drawn carriages to the ghostly whispers after dark. General Oglethorpe lies here, as well as some 10,000 settlers and soldiers from the 1700s and 1800s. The imposing arch was a gift from the Daughters of the American Revolution.

Summertime Beauty

The gnarled trunk of the crape myrtle tree yields the showiest of summertime flowers. Savannah's combination of soil and rainfall create ideal conditions for the crape myrtle's beautiful pink, white, red, and lavender blossoms. When they're finished, the colorful blossoms blanket the ground below.

Winged Lion (above)

This regal five-foot tall terra cotta lion, circa 1889, guards the Old Savannah Cotton Exchange. Nineteenth-Century cotton brokers were called factors; thus the name of the cobblestone passage between the Bay Street and the River: Factor's Walk.

Cotton Exchange (opposite)

Eli Whitney invented the cotton gin on a plantation near Savannah in 1793, and soon afterward, Savannah was exporting more than two million bales of cotton a year. Even before the construction of the historic Cotton Exchange in 1887, the city was setting the world prices for cotton here along Factor's Walk.

Wrought Iron and Spanish Moss *(above)*

If you can't see any wrought iron or even a tendril of Spanish moss from where you're standing, check your map. You may not be in Savannah. Much of Savannah's notable ironwork came from the forge of Ivan Bailey, who lived here in the 1970s.

Old City Exchange Bell *(opposite)*

When the original wooden City Exchange building was razed, the beautiful bell, which had been cast in Amsterdam, was saved. It eventually was placed in a specially built replica of the original cupola in front of the Chamber of Commerce building near the Old Cotton Exchange.

Spanish Moss

Not a moss at all, but a perennial herb, this ethereal, Gothic-looking air plant has a particular preference for live oak trees. Draped from the treetops like a lacy beard, Spanish moss can grow as long as 20 feet.

State Tree of Georgia

The live oak, with its low, undulating branches, is beloved by artists, photographers, and children who love to climb. Besides the cool shade it affords for picnics, its extremely hard wood was prized in the shipbuilding industry. The *U.S.S. Constitution* (*Old Ironsides*) was made of live oak.

Gothic to Victorian *(above)*

Aesthetic detailing from the Romantic movement of the 1800s is reflected in a diversity of architectural styles that stand in graceful coexistence throughout Historic Savannah. The elegant window casements give this Gaston Street home a Neo-gothic flavor.

The Gingerbread House *(opposite)*

This ornate home at 1921 Bull Street is the most photographed Victorian era structure in Savannah. Its elaborate façade of arches and curlicues literally stops traffic as amazed passersby slow to point cameras from their cars. President Franklin D. Roosevelt reportedly halted the 1933 Bicentennial parade to get a closer look.

Dappled Light *(opposite)*

Savannah's trademark dappled light, romantic under blue skies and ethereal by moon glow, is a natural phenomenon caused by the canopies of oak trees feathered with Spanish moss.

Hamilton-Turner House *(above)*

This 1873 Second Empire mansion plays prominently in *Midnight in the Garden of Good and Evil*, as the infamous Odom party house. It also was the first home in the city to have electricity. The stately French style home has emerged from many incarnations to become one of Savannah's most luxurious bed and breakfast inns.

Mercer Williams House *(above)*

Though designed for the great-grandfather of songwriter Johnny Mercer, the Mercer family never occupied this home. In 1969 preservationist Jim Williams purchased it and spent two years restoring it. Later, Williams became the central figure in *Midnight in the Garden of Good and Evil.* The home is open for tours.

No Two Alike *(opposite)*

Whether they're purebred Queen Anne, Greek Revival, English Regency, Federal, Romanesque Revival, Gothic Revival, Italianate, or a charming mix, Savannah's thousands of period-style homes reflect a charm that's part Old South, part Old World and part old fashioned graciousness.

Natural Arches *(above)*

Architecture in Savannah is hardly limited
to building design, as evidenced by the
trellises, privet gardens and hand-trained
garden arches. One of Savannah's most
glorious events is its annual Spring Tour
of Homes and Gardens, when visitors get
more than a peek through the hedges or
a glimpse through a window.

Gaston Street *(opposite)*

One of the most beautiful streets in all
of Savannah is Gaston, where storybook-
perfect wooden Victorian homes and
stately stone and stucco mansions make
perfect neighbors. With its tower and cupola,
arches, and delightful combination of
window designs, this private home always
inspires a second glance.

Living History at Davenport House

The authentically restored 1820s Federal style mansion and lush gardens of the Davenport House Museum feature period décor, candlelight tours, and living history dramatizations.

Savannah Revived

The tragic decay of many architectural treasures prompted Lady Astor, on a visit to the city in 1946, to call Savannah "a beautiful lady with a dirty face." The condition of the Davenport House inspired the formation of the Historic Savannah Foundation, setting in motion the restoration of Old Savannah to its former grandeur.

Davenport House Gardens *(above and opposite)*

The beautiful gardens of the Davenport House reflect the work of noted horticulturist Penelope Hobhouse. Located at 324 East State Street on Columbia Square, the Davenport House is a popular spot for private receptions and social gatherings.

Owens-Thomas House *(above and opposite)*

Considered by some architecture historians to be the finest example of English Regency architecture in America, this William Jay-designed stucco-over-tabby home at 124 Abercorn Street features stunning gardens, a brass inlaid staircase and an intact slave house. Now a museum, it is owned by the Telfair Museum of Art.

Green-Meldrim House *(top)*

Here, in the home of cotton merchant
Charles Green, General Sherman ended his
300-mile March to the Sea and dispatched
his famous telegram to President Lincoln: *"I
beg to present to you, as a Christmas gift the
city of Savannah, with one hundred and fifty
guns and plenty of ammunition, and also
about twenty-five thousand bales of cotton."*

Olde Pink House Restaurant *(bottom)*

One of Savannah's loveliest restaurants is
also among its most historic homes. Built in
1771 on Reynolds Square for a cotton
planter, the pink stucco-over-brick Georgian-
style mansion was the site of secret strategic
meetings for the independence of the 13
colonies. Later the headquarters for Georgia's
first bank, its vault is now a wine cellar.

Wishing Pond

This charming fish fountain delights parishioners and guests at the Green-Meldrim House, which now serves as the Parish House for St. John's Episcopal Church. The house, located at 14 West Macon Street on Madison Square, is an exceptional example of Neo-Gothic architecture by John Norris. It opens for tours several days a week.

Savannah Grey Brick *(top)*

You won't find authentic Savannah Grey Brick in your architectural supply catalog. Manufactured in Savannah in the 1800s, the coveted pink-tinged, grey brick can be seen in hundreds of old homes, restaurants, and inns, either exposed or peeking out from centuries-old stucco walls like this one.

Massie School *(bottom)*

The only remaining building in Georgia's original public school system, this John Norris-designed Greek Revival building closed as a free school for the poor in 1974 and became the Massie Heritage Center. It houses a 3-D model of the entire Savannah Landmark Historic District as well as priceless photos of now-demolished homes.

Flannery O'Connor Home *(opposite)*

207 E. Charleton Street was the birthplace of this icon of Southern literature, who produced an enduring body of work before her early death at age 39. The recently-renovated home hosts a variety of literary events.

Carriage Rides *(above)*

There's a timeless cadence to the history and charm of Savannah that perfectly complements the gentle motion of a horse and carriage as it meanders along cobblestone streets, beneath the canopy of majestic oaks.

Ballastone Inn *(opposite)*

Nowhere is Southern hospitality more present than in the historic bed and breakfast inns of Savannah. One of the loveliest is the Ballastone Inn at 14 East Oglethorpe, next door to the Juliette Low Birthplace.

Dogwoods in Springtime *(top)*

When the snowy-white blooms of the dogwood trees coincide with the blooming of the azaleas, and both the camellias and the daffodils still linger in shady places, it's a perfect spring day in Savannah.

Sorrel-Weed House *(bottom)*

This massive Greek Revival mansion with Regency influence, circa 1840, is one of the most talked-about historic buildings in Savannah. A sordid history and reports of ghostly sightings have brought in paranormal researchers from around the world.

Historic Cobblestones

Among the oldest artifacts of Colonial Georgia are the cobblestones along River Street and around the historic cotton warehouses on Factor's Walk. These multi-toned, irregular stones came from England over 250 years ago as ballast in the holds of sailing ships that brought the first colonists to Savannah.

Wisteria and Victoriana

Cupolas, ornate millwork, gables, and stained glass windows are hallmarks of the Victorian period. A perfect example is Chestnut House, circa 1897, cloaked here in her springtime show of wisteria.

Gingerbread Stroll

Savannah's Victorian District is lined with pastel homes laced with creamy, hand-milled "gingerbread" trim. Verandahs appointed with wicker-and-chintz furniture, secret gardens and the fragrance of Confederate jasmine make Savannah a wonderful city for strolling.

Juliette Gordon Low Birthplace

This garden, at 10 East Oglethorpe belonged to the John Norris-designed home of William Washington Gordon, who founded the Central of Georgia Railroad. However, the home is best remembered for his granddaughter, Juliette "Daisy" Gordon, founder the Girl Scouts of America.

Beloved Daisy Gordon

Girl Scouts from around the world make the pilgrimage to Savannah to tour Daisy Gordon's birthplace, which is now a National Center for Girl Scouts of America, as well as a National Historic Landmark. The site hosts Girl Scout events, celebrations, and public tours featuring many Gordon family pieces, including Daisy's own artwork.

Stairway to River Street

Stone steps and cobblestone ramps leading from the park-like setting on Factor's Walk above, to River Street below, were designed for the use of sailors and seaport workers. The quaint staircases add to the ambience that belongs only to Savannah.

Architectural Accents

Oversize 19th-century planters can be seen throughout Historic Savannah, standing sentry at grand entrances and overflowing with flowers in secret gardens. During the winter, while they rest, they make great roosting spots for pigeons.

Waving Girl (above and opposite)

Florence Martus, isolated on an island in 1887, began waving to passing ships. Some say she mourned her sailor who went to sea and never returned. For 44 years, she waved, and each ship sounded its horn in greeting. A bronze statue of Florence stands at the east end of River Street, where passing ships still respectfully sound their horns.

Friendly Rivalry (above)

Charleston, South Carolina's Arthur Ravenel, Jr. Bridge bears a strong resemblance to Savannah's 1.9-mile cable-stayed Talmadge Memorial Bridge, named for former governor Eugene Talmadge. Savannahians point out that theirs came first.

Slave Statue (opposite)

Most slaves were brought into Georgia through the Savannah seaport, so it was fitting that a memorial to their struggle should be placed on the riverfront. In 2002, the City of Savannah dedicated this Dorothy Spradley-designed bronze statue depicting a family in broken chains, with a poignant inscription by Maya Angelou.

Strolling and Shopping

Old brick warehouses along the waterfront that once housed the wholesale cotton trade are now an eclectic mix of antique stores, clothing boutiques, art galleries, gift shops, hotels, and residences. This promenade on the upper level is called Factor's Walk. Below are the restaurants, shops, and galleries of River Street.

First Sights

For more than two centuries, the first glimpse of Savannah by international cargo ships has included the golden dome of City Hall, the Old Cotton Exchange, and its cotton warehouses along River Street. Today, the seamen share their views of Savannah's busy port with sightseers on picturesque paddleboats.

Music on River Street

It's not unusual in Savannah for musicians
to hear the call and break into a tune on
River Street or any park bench throughout
the Historic District.

The Savannah River Queen

Savannah's Riverboat Cruises offers moonlight cruises, luncheon cruises, Gospel dinner cruises, murder mystery cruises, and more aboard charming red, white, and blue-swagged triple-decker stern-wheel boats.

Black Skimmers

Most common to the beaches of Blackbeard Island and Wassaw National Wildlife Refuge, Black Skimmers, Laughing Gulls, and other seabirds occasionally make their way up the Savannah River. Easily identified by their rich breeding plumage, they glide low over shallow water in search of small fish and crustaceans.

Crossing the Savannah

One way to cross the Savannah River to Hutchinson Island's Savannah International Trade & Convention Center is by water taxi. The Savannah Belles Ferry vessels are named for two "belles," Girl Scouts Founder Juliette Gordon Low and Susie King Taylor, a freed slave who became a nurse and teacher.

Historic Custom House

One of eight official, Historic Custom Houses in America, this impressive marble and granite building was designed by John Norris in the 1840s when it quartered the Custom Services, The Post Office, and the Federal Court. Today, it is managed by the General Services Administration.

24-Karat City Hall

With its ornate granite and limestone Renaissance Revival design, its 24-karat gold-plated copper dome, and its four 7-foot clock dials, Savannah's City Hall, built in 1901, is as much an architectural treasure as it is the seat of municipal government.

Temple Mickve Israel *(opposite)*

Consecrated in 1878, Temple Mickve Israel on Monterey Square reflects the gothic architecture of the Victorian era. Its most notable treasure is the 15th century Torah brought to Savannah by the early settlers. The 42 sunrays on the crest of the Congregation Mickve Israel represent Savannah's 42 original Jewish settlers.

Cathedral of St. John the Baptist *(above)*

The soaring twin spires of this Gothic-style Roman Catholic Church create a dramatic view of the city from I-16. The cathedral's awe-inspiring interiors include newly refurbished stained glass windows and murals. The cathedral overlooks Lafayette Square.

First African Baptist Church

One of the oldest continuous Black congregations in America worships here at the oldest standing brick church building in Georgia. Located on Franklin Square, some of its original pews have made by the African slaves. The church was an active haven on the Underground Railroad.

Touring Savannah

Ghostly spirit tours, "The Book" tours, moonlight and champagne tours, Girl Scout tours, history tours, cemetery tours, gastronomical tours, Victoriana tours, and museum tours… the choices are endless. One simply cannot visit Savannah without at least one carriage ride, either on a group tour or a private booking.

City Market *(above)*

One of the liveliest and most romantic sections of Old Savannah lies between two of Savannah's original squares at Jefferson and West Saint Julian Streets. City Market encompasses four blocks of restored grain warehouses, which now house cafés, art galleries, restaurants, and shops.

Rotary Centennial *(opposite)*

Savannah's six Rotary clubs recently presented this 15-foot "fancy street clock" to the city to commemorate the Rotary Centennial.

State Flower of Georgia *(above)*

If there's a sister to the steel magnolia—a term used to represent the beauty and strength of Southern women—it is perhaps the Cherokee Rose, a soft but prickly and tenacious climbing rose bush named in honor of the Cherokee Nation.

Bird Girl *(opposite)*

Savannah's best-known 20th-century sculpture is *Bird Girl*, a bronze piece by Sylvia Shaw Judson. Once a private monument at Bonaventure Cemetery, she was made so famous on the cover of *Midnight in the Garden of Good and Evil* that she had to be relocated to the Telfair Museum for safekeeping.

WE ARE CONFIDENT, I SAY,
AND WILLING RATHER TO
BE ABSENT FROM THE BODY,
AND TO BE PRESENT WITH
THE LORD. II CORINTHIANS 5:8

Beach Institute *(left)*

Built in 1867 by the Freedmen's Bureau, this school for African American children at 502 East Harris Street remained in operation until 1919. It now is the headquarters of the King-Tisdell Cottage Foundation, which hosts lectures, exhibits, and events.

Oldest African-American Community *(right)*

The Ralph Mark Gilbert Civil Rights Museum, named for the renowned Civil Rights and NAACP leader, chronicles Savannah's African American community from slavery to present. Originally The Wage Earners Saving and Loan Bank for Black Savannahians, the largest African American bank in the U.S, it has an exceptional photographic collection.

Jepson Museum (top)

The newest building in the Telfair trilogy, this state-of the art museum features 20th- and 21st-century art, and includes ArtZeum, a dynamic interactive museum for children. Outdoor sculpture terraces offer lovely views of Telfair Square and Historic Savannah.

Big Name Entertainment (bottom)

Broadway, ballet, circus, concert, or Monster Truck exhibition—all of these and about 900 events more take place at The Savannah Civic Center, with its arena and theater that can seat up to 12,000 people. The Civic Center is located at the corner of Liberty and Montgomery Streets.

Fort Pulaski *(opposite, top)*

Guarding the mouth of the Savannah River, Fort Pulaski is a classic example of 19th-century military architecture, complete with a picturesque moat and drawbridge, and ramparts which afford panoramic views of the marshes and Tybee Island.

Military Might *(opposite, bottom)*

Named for Revolutionary War hero Casimir Pulaski, this largely intact fortification built with 25 million bricks was considered impenetrable. That changed when Union forces introduced the rifled cannon during the Civil War, rendering brick fortifications obsolete.

Artifacts of War *(above)*

This type of field cannon, positioned just inside the fort's walls, would be a last line of defense against invaders who managed to slip past the larger cannons aimed at approaching ships. Every Saturday, history comes alive at Fort Pulaski with hourly cannon firings and demonstrations.

Fort McAllister

Live oak trees, salt marsh vistas, hiking and cycling trails, camping sites, stilt cottages, fishing, and a boat ramp make this State Historic Park worth the 20-mile drive southeast of Savannah.

Earthwork Fortification

Strategically built on the banks of the Great Ogeechee River, Fort McAllister is the best-preserved earthwork fortification of the Confederacy. The park has a fine museum with interactive exhibits.

Old Fort Jackson

Old Fort Jackson, named for Georgia governor and Revolutionary War soldier James Jackson, is Georgia's oldest brick fort. It protected Savannah during the War of 1812 and held off the Union forces until Sherman's March to the Sea.

Casemates

The heavily fortified vaulted casemates, or artillery storage chambers, have withstood the ravages of time at Old Fort Jackson. The casemates now house exhibits of artillery and other artifacts of war.

Wormsloe Plantation

Some of Savannah's earliest settlers were sent to the Isle of Hope to guard a back-river entrance to Savannah. Noble Jones, one of the first 114 British colonists who arrived with General Oglethorpe, built an impressive, fortified plantation house. He named it Wormsloe. The 1.5-mile avenue from the entry gate to the plantation ruins is lined with 400 live oak trees.

Living History *(top and bottom)*

Each February, Wormsloe Historic Site (7601 Skidaway Road) hosts the Colonial Faire and Muster, a colorful weekend of living history, arts and crafts, military formations, and musket firings.

Tabby Ruins *(opposite, top)*

The abundance of oyster shell middens along the Georgia coast led to the widespread use of tabby construction. Tabby is a concrete material made of sand, limestone, crushed oyster shells, and water. The construction of Wormsloe Plantation required 8,000 bushels of tabby.

Wormsloe Historic Site *(opposite, bottom)*

Managed by Georgia Department of Natural Resources, the 1200-acre site encompasses nature trails, picnic areas, the tabby ruins, and a museum. A permit is required to visit the adjacent barrier islands. Wormsloe is on the Colonial Birding Trail. The annual Colonial Christmas includes 18th-century caroling, dance, and the burning of the Yule log.

Savannah History Museum *(above)*

A perfect introduction to the rich history of Savannah is found in the old Central of Georgia Railroad train shed, now home of the Savannah History Museum. The open atmosphere of the museum invites visitors to view more than 10,000 artifacts from 1733 to today.

Roundhouse Railroad Museum
(above and opposite)

The old Central of Georgia Railway Station was built on the site of the 1779 Revolutionary War Battle of Savannah. Though no longer an active train depot, it still houses locomotives and train cars, and they still fire up the oldest portable steam engine in the U.S. A massive turntable moves train cars around.

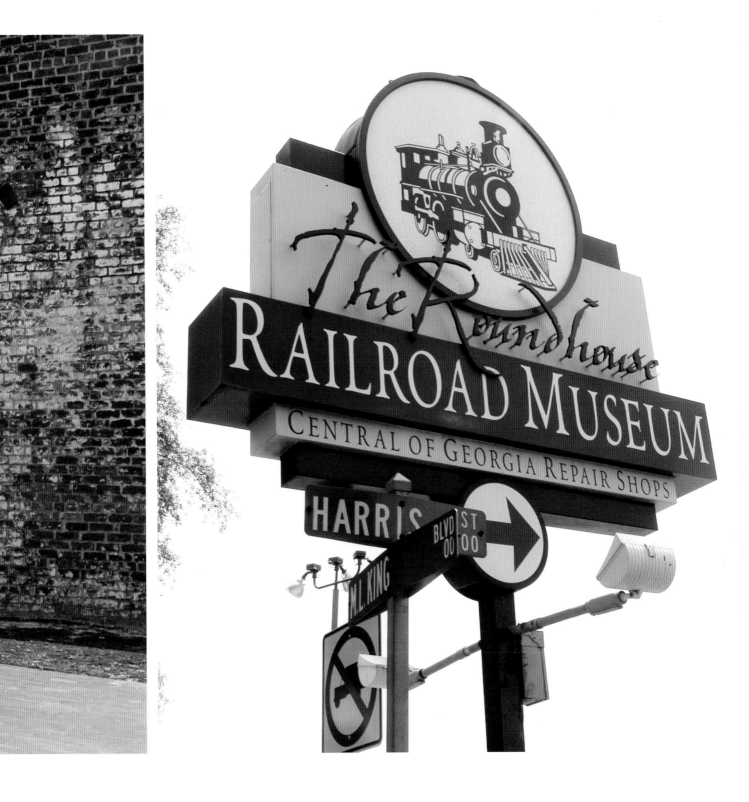

Roundhouse Smokestack *(opposite)*

This gothic-style smokestack, with its 125-foot tower and cast-iron cistern, is among the original buildings still standing on the historic site. The ground level houses privies built for railroad crews.

Love Affair with History *(above)*

Beyond their love of fine period antiques, architecture, and art, Savannahians have a deep respect for even the simplest artifacts reflecting the city's rich cultural history. Fresh flowers breathe new life into this old carriage on the grounds of the old Central of Georgia Railway Station.

Ships of the Sea Museum *(top)*

Mr. William Scarbrough, president of the Savannah Steamship Company, would surely be pleased to know that his home has become the Ships of the Sea Maritime Museum, showcasing the seafaring history of the 18th and 19th centuries, and particularly Savannah's contribution to maritime history. Pictured is a wheelhouse from an 1859 English tugboat.

Extraordinary Ship Models *(bottom)*

The museum collection includes maritime antiques, paintings, and artifacts, as well as models of some of the famous ships in seafaring history. A most-treasured model (not shown), is the *Savannah*, of which Mr. Scarbrough was a principal owner. She was a fully-rigged sailing frigate with a steam engine —the first steamship to cross the Atlantic.

Scarbrough House

Even before it became home to the Ships of the Sea Maritime Museum, the William Scarbrough House was distinguished as one of the most stunning examples of Greek Revival architecture in America. The home, at 41 MLK, Jr. Blvd., is also noted for its authentic 19th-century parlor garden— the largest garden in the Historic District.

Education, Restoration, and Adaptation
(above and opposite)

The young but distinguished Savannah College of Art and Design, affectionately called SCAD, uses historic buildings for its widespread campus. It currently has saved, restored, and/or adapted at least 60 buildings throughout the Historic and Victorian Districts.

Movie Set Campus *(opposite, top)*

The 173-acre marsh-side campus of Savannah State University reflects a vibrant blending of state-of-the-art education and gracious antebellum architecture. Bernard Hill Hall, built in 1901, was used in the filming of the movie, *The General's Daughter.*

Savannah State University *(opposite, bottom)*

Savannah State University is the oldest public historically Black college in Georgia. It was established as a result of the Second Morrill Land Grant Act in 1890. Several of the buildings, including Adams Hall, were built by students and faculty members to reflect period architecture.

Clear as A Bell *(above)*

While the history of this century-old bell at Bernard Hill Hall is hazy, and it chimes are—at least temporarily—silent, its value as a beloved landmark on the Savannah State University campus is very clear.

Wild Georgia Shrimp *(top)*

Shrimping is still an important industry here on Savannah's coast. Chances are the crew of these boats already have retired for the night, so they will be rested for their pre-dawn departure for the open waters of the Atlantic.

Return of the Shrimpers *(bottom)*

Gulls follow the shrimp boat *Yellow* as she rounds the Cockspur Island Lighthouse with a hold full of bounty. The island is at the mouth of the Savannah River, which feeds into the Atlantic.

Bird Watching

The flight of egrets is a common sight throughout the Savannah coastal region, and particularly so at the Savannah National Wildlife Refuge. Operated by the U.S. Fish and Wildlife Service, this 28,000-acre refuge is home to a variety of wildlife including several endangered or threatened species.

Bull River *(above)*

Winding through salt marshes and tidal creeks is Bull River, a beautiful stretch of the Intracoastal Waterway. Public boat launching spots and river cruise companies can be found just off Old Tybee Road near Wilmington Island.

A People-Refuge, Too *(opposite)*

Straddling Georgia and South Carolina, the Savannah National Wildlife Refuge, less than 30 minutes from Savannah near Port Wentworth, offers respite from the world, not just for birds and wildlife, but also for the visitors who view the land and waterscapes from the Laurel Hill Wildlife Drive.

Rivers and Creeks

Savannahians savor nothing more than
their instant access to water, whether it's
to toss a line off the dock, or to slip away
for a day of boating in the creeks and
rivers. Dozens of outfitters offer guided
tours and private charters.

Evening Marsh

Despite its serene appearance, the marsh is teeming with fish and wildlife. The mucky sand bottom nurtures oyster beds and crabs, while the tall grasses provide rich nesting and feeding grounds for a variety of seabirds. So lush and green in summer, the marsh turns golden brown in winter.

Sunset over Moon River

Originally known simply as The Back River, Savannah's famous son Johnny Mercer changed its name forever with his song, "Moon River." Mercer once had a home on this beautiful river, which he and co-lyricist Henry Mancini immortalized in the theme song for *Breakfast at Tiffany's*.

Wider Than A Mile

Moon River is a rich refuge for the bird and sea-life along Savannah's marshy coast. Photogenic old pilings, jetties and palmetto hammocks, as well as excellent fishing, draw sportsmen, boaters, and photographers to find the "rainbow's end … waitin' 'round the bend," as the lyrics promise.

Skidaway Island (top)

Skidaway Island is a rare balance of luxury real estate and unspoiled wilderness. Original inhabitants, 40,000 years ago, were mammoths, ground sloths, and mastodons. Since then, island residents have included British settlers, plantation owners, bootleggers, and more recently, The Landings on Skidaway Island, a luxury golf community.

Territorial Rights (bottom)

Alligators live in swampy areas around rivers, creeks, and ponds. Skidaway Island State Park and The Savannah National Wildlife Refuge are great places for sensational sightings, but visitors are warned to keep a respectful distance.

Gone Fishin'

No longer quite suitable for a fishing excursion of the human kind, picturesque sunken boats like this one on Lazaretto Creek make perfect vantage points for hungry herons, egrets, and other sea birds.

Skidaway Island State Park (*opposite*)

The 588-acre Skidaway Island State Park offers camping, hiking, picnic and playground facilities, and stunning marsh and water views from the observation towers.

Natural Beauty (*above*)

Just eight miles long and three miles wide, Skidaway Island is protected from the Atlantic Ocean by the barrier islands of Wassaw, Ossabaw, and Tybee. Kayakers and canoers are drawn to the island for its unspoiled, wildlife-abundant saltwater estuaries.

Tybee Light

Among the prettiest lighthouses on the Atlantic coast, the 154-foot-tall Tybee Light can be seen 18 miles out to sea. Both the original wooden 1736 lighthouse and the second one, of wood and stone, washed out to sea. The interior of the third was deliberately burned by the Confederates to prevent the Yankees from access.

Palmetto and Palm

Designed by nature to thrive in dry sand and salt air, the Sabal palm and scrub palmetto are common throughout the Savannah landscape. From fan-like accents around Victorian mansions to towering sentries like this one near the Tybee Light, some of this native flora dates back to Colonial days.

Peerless Pier *(above)*

Though serene at sunrise and at sunset, the restored Tybee Pier and its predecessors have been the vibrant center of beach life since the turn of the 20th century. Fishing is free from both the pier and the beach.

South Channel Light *(opposite)*

Georgia's smallest lighthouse, just 46 feet tall, sits on an oyster bed off Cockspur Island, home of the Fort Pulaski National Monument. It was here that "waving girl" Frances Martus lived with her brother, light keeper George Washington Martus. She actually waved from her porch on Elba Island next door.

Work or Play?

These skimmers could be frolicking in the sand like any other beach-goer, but more than likely they are defending a nest in the sand by making lines around it with their long bills. When a Black Skimmer is frightened, it sometimes digs itself a sandy hiding place.

Sugary White Dunes

Sensitive to the ebb and flow of beach erosion, and protective of its nesting birds, the town of Tybee has built a network of boardwalks to protect vulnerable sand dunes.

Debbi Zepp

Debbi Zepp captures Savannah's diverse beauty in her breathtaking photographs. Through her eyes, Debbi takes you on a tour of Southern history, coastal waters, wildlife, marshes, architecture, and character that only Savannah, Georgia, offers. She invites you to experience Coastal Georgia, where she resides, *"… to take in all the beauty a soul needs to be happy."*

Born and raised in Bethesda, Maryland, Debbi has been a newspaper photojournalist in the D.C. area, photographer and graphic designer in Lexington, Kentucky, and an award-winning photographer in Coastal Georgia. She has traveled and lived on and off the Continent, including Guam, where her son Jonz was born. Debbi's photographs are available in Savannah galleries and at art shows throughout the year, and she's always looking for one more bird, wildlife, landscape or seascape to photograph. It keeps her creative.

To view more of Debbi Zepp's photography please visit www.zeptek.com.